Contents

D1324768

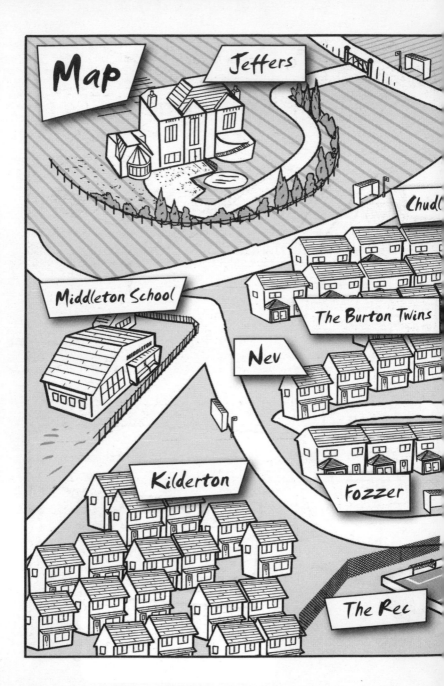

Meet the Jags

Andy

Name: Andrew Burton

Fact: He's the Jags' captain.

Loves: Spurs

FYI: The Jags may be his mates, but they'd better not forget he's the Skipper.

Burts

Name: Terry Burton

Fact: He's Andy's twin brother.

Loves: Football, football, and more football. He's football crazy!

FYI: He's a big Arsenal fan.

Dev

Name: Ryan Devlin

Fact: He's very forgetful.

Loves: Daydreaming!

FYI: He's always covered in mud and bruises.

Fozzer

Name: Hamed Foster

Fact: He can run like crazy, but he shoots like crazy too – sometimes at the wrong goal!

Loves: Telling bad jokes.

FYI: His best friend is Nev.

Keeps

Name: Jim Ward

Fact: He's the Jags' Number One goalie – whether he likes it or not!

Loves: Trying to score from his end of the pitch.

FYI: He's the tallest member of the Jags.

Jeffers

Name: Jeffrey Gilfoyle Chapman

Fact: He's the only one of the Jags who doesn't live on the Chudley Park estate.

Loves: Being in the Jags.

FYI: He's the Jags' top goal-scorer.

Name: Denton Neville

Fact: Nev is the Jags' most talented player.

Loves: Fozzer's bad jokes.

FYI: He keeps his feet on the ground and always looks out for his football crazy mates.

Mrs Burton

Name: Pam Burton

Fact: The Burton twins' mum, and a team 'mum' for all the Jags.

Loves: Sorting out her boys.

FYI: Doesn't actually like football!

Mr Ward

Name: Jack Ward

Fact: He's Jim's dad and the Jags' coach!

Loves: Going on and on, doing his team talks.

FYI: He's taking his coaching exams.

Home Time

Sometimes I wish my brother Andy and I went to the same school. Other times, I'm really glad he's at Middleton and I'm at Parkside.

Andy   Hi, Burts. Why are you walking like that?

Burts   Look. The bottom's come off my shoe.

Andy   Mum's not going to be happy, bruv.

Burts   Well, it wasn't my fault. It just came unstuck.

Andy   It just came unstuck all on its own?

Burts   Well, we *were* playing football at break-time. But even so. They should make them stronger.

Andy   So what are you going to do, then, bruv?

Burts   Have we got any glue left? Or did you use it all up to fix the water blaster?

Andy   I think there's some left. I used quite a lot, though, because my shoes came apart last week, too.

Burts   Maybe it's Mum's fault for buying cheap shoes in the sale.

Andy   I don't think she'll see it that way, Burts.

Burts   No, I know. Anyway, did the glue work on yours?

Andy   Yeah. But it took a lot of glue. That's why there's not much left.

Burts   Will you do me a favour?

Andy   I will if you say Spurs are better
than Arsenal.

Burts   Never. Just do me a favour. Keep
Mum talking when we get in.
I'll run upstairs before she sees
what's happened.

Andy   Anything for you, bruv.

Burts   Thanks, Andy.

Andy   No problem. There's just one thing, though.

Burts   What's that?

Andy   Spurs *are* better than Arsenal! By a mile!

Finished Your Homework?

We got home and I fixed my shoe. Then we went out into the back garden. Mum called out: "Have you two finished your homework already?"

Andy   Almost, Mum. I'll finish it after tea.

Burts   Have you really almost done
your homework?

Andy   Um, no!

Burts   Oh, well, let's play until tea's
ready.

Andy   Okay. Let's play one against
one.

Burts   And Theo Walcott hits it first time. It must be a goal.

Andy   But, no. Gareth Bale clears off the line. And they are on the attack. Oops!

Burts   And it's into next door's garden. The Spurs man will have to go round and ask for the ball back.

All that fuss about my brother's shoe made me forget the big news.

Burts Have you got the ball back?

Andy Yeah, here it is.

Burts Come on, then. You kicked it over so it's my ball.

Andy Wait a minute, Burts. I wanted to ask you about the school match. Parkside against Middleton.

Burts What school match? When?

Andy   Next Friday after school.

Burts   Nobody's said anything about it at our school. I don't even know who will be in the team.

Andy   You'd better find out, mate.

Burts   Why? We'll beat you anyway. We always do!

Andy   You wish! Come on. Let's go and see what's for tea.

Game On!

Middleton against Parkside would be a derby match, like Arsenal against Spurs, or Liverpool against Everton. But what about the Jags? Half of us play for one school, half for the other. Andy and I got to the Rec early for training.

Burts   Do the others all know about the school match?

Andy   I told Fozzer and Nev today.

Burts   Dev knows. And Keeps knows about everything.

Andy   Do you think he'll be in goal for you?

Burts   I don't know. It's not up to me.
I bet he'll want to play up front.
Another boy goes in goal for
our school sometimes. But he's
not as good as Keeps.

Andy   Come on, give me the ball. Let's
play against the wall. It's good
for your control.

Burts   Do you remember what
happened last time your school
played my school?

Andy   Yes. We beat you, of course.

Burts   I don't mean that. I mean it was funny playing against other Jags. Do you remember when Dev fouled Nev? They had a big argument.

Andy   Yeah, I remember. They didn't talk for weeks, did they?

Burts Exactly. Nev refused to play for the Jags. We were a man short for two games.

Andy It's all right now, isn't it? That was ages ago.

Burts But you know what derby matches are like. There's always trouble in those games.

Andy   If Dev and Nev have another argument, we could lose our best player.

Burts   Exactly. I think you should talk to the others about it. You are the Jags' skipper, after all.

Andy   Yeah. I could do it after training. Let's finish off this game. Was it 3–2 to me?

Rivals!

So, after training, Andy did what he said. He gave us a team talk.

Andy   This game between our schools will be fun, as long as there are no fouls or arguments. The Jags have got a big game two days later.

Burts   That's right, Skipper. Our schools only play each other once a year. The Jags play every week. We want the Jags to be the best team in Kilderton. So we need to stay mates, don't we?

Andy   We will, Burts. You wait and see.

I was really worried about the school match. On the day, I was captain of Middleton. Burts was captain of Parkside.

Burts Good luck, bruv. Don't get too down when we beat you!

Andy We're going to win! Your only chance is that the ref's a teacher from your school!

Andy Come on, Middleton. Get the ball forward.

Burts Come on, Parkside. Let's win the ball and head for goal.

Andy Great pass, Nev.

Burts Good tackle, Dev. Send it up the wing.

Andy Unlucky, Nev. Let's get the ball back off them.

I got the ball in midfield. Just as I was about to pass, CRUNCH! Someone slid in from behind me. It really hurt!

Andy   I got the ball, ref!

Burts   Ow! You idiot, Andy. You were nowhere near the ball. That really hurt.

Andy   I got the ball. It was a good tackle.

Burts   No, it wasn't. You got my ankle before you got the ball. That's a bad foul.

Andy   Oh, why don't you stop moaning?

Burts   I'll make you stop moaning if you're not careful.

Andy   Yeah? I'd like to see you try.

Burts   Come on, then. I don't care if
you *are* my brother.

I was really angry. So was
Burts. Mr Rogers made us
both go and calm down.
The game finished 1–1.
When we got home, we still
weren't talking. What
about the Jags game?
Would we make up in time?

Team Spirit

The Jags against Hillcrest was on Sunday. Andy and I were still not talking.

Andy   Burts?

Burts   What?

Andy   Does your leg still hurt?

Burts   It's still really bruised.

Andy	Let me see. Can you still play today?
Burts	I don't know. Here, look.
Andy	I can't see anything.
Burts	Oh. It must be the other leg.

Andy   It can't be too bad if you don't know which leg it is!

Burts   I suppose not. But I'm still angry with you.

Andy   Are you too angry to play for the Jags today?

Burts   Let me think …
What are you talking about? I'd have to have a broken leg not to play today!

I felt like giving Burts a hug. But he's my brother, so I didn't. I mean, I like him. But not that much. Anyway, we went to meet the others for the game.

Burts   It's all right, everybody. Andy said sorry.

Andy   I suppose it was up to me. I did the foul. If it *was* a foul, that is.

Burts   Anyway, it's all in the past. So we can get on with winning today.

Andy It's nearly half-time. Let's try and take the lead. Start running, Burts.

Burts I'm free in the area, Andy.

Andy Here it comes. Past the defender.

Burts Got it! Van Persie shoots. He scores!

Andy And the Jags are winning 1–0!

Burts   Not a bad pass, bruv!

Andy   We won't argue about that.

Burts   And not a bad shot, eh?

Andy   We won't argue about that,
either!

Burts   Right. Let's get this game won.

Andy   Come on the Jags!
and Burts

JAGUARS 3 HILLCREST 3

That game against Hillcrest was one of the best of the season. I got us back to 1–1. Then Hillcrest hit us on the break to put us 2–1 down.

Andy Oh, no! That striker's in on goal again. Can Keeps stop him?

Burts No chance. Unlucky, Keeps. What now, Andy? That's 3–1 to them.

Burts   Get it forward to Jeffers. But
keep passing, lads!

Andy   Well played, Jeffers!

Burts   That's 3–2 to Hillcrest. We can
do this, Jags!

Andy I'm okay at the back on my own. Everybody get forward. We have to get another goal!

Burts Good idea. Pass it to me, Andy.

Andy Nev's making a run, bruv!

Burts All he needs is the ball. And he scores! Yes! What a comeback!

Ouch!

 Every footballer knows what it's like to get injured. Sometimes, you twist your ankle but you play on. If you get badly injured, you have to leave the pitch and a sub comes on.

 Sometimes players break a leg in a game. Others break little bones in their feet. A torn muscle is a bad injury. You can't see the injury from outside but it really hurts. And it can take ages to get better.

The person who looks after injured players is called a physiotherapist. The physio is at the game to treat any injuries, and helps players to get better afterwards, too.

At big clubs, they have a doctor at the game. The doctor can run on and check any injuries. If the player can't walk, he goes off on a stretcher. Sometimes he has to go to hospital for a check-up.

Ouch! Quiz

Questions

1 What is the bend in your leg called?

2 What injury can happen to a player's foot?

3 What kind of injury happens to muscles?

4 Why can a player keep playing if he hurts his hand in a game?

5 Who looks after injured players?

Answers

5 The physio.
4 Because he uses his foot to kick the ball.
3 They get torn.
2 Broken bone.
1 Knee.

About the Author

Tom Watt, who wrote the Jags books, used to love playing football. He used to play 50 or 60 games every year. But he had to stop when he got a bad injury. He tore a ligament in his knee. It took ages to get better. The doctor told him not to play again.

So Tom stopped playing. Well, almost. He still kicks a ball around with his son most days. But he's really careful. If you ever see Tom's doctor, don't tell him about football in the back garden, will you?

THE JAGS

Who's Got My Boots?

A New Striker

The Derby Match

Who's Washing the Kit?

The Big Deal

Star Player Wanted

Your Turn in Goal

The Team Talk

Whose Side Are You On?

Hitting the Headlines

Up for the Cup

The Own Goal